AMONG PYTHON

AF424434

OMPRAKASH

Copyright © Omprakash
All Rights Reserved.

This book has been self-published with all reasonable efforts taken to make the material error-free by the author. No part of this book shall be used, reproduced in any manner whatsoever without written permission from the author, except in the case of brief quotations embodied in critical articles and reviews.

The Author of this book is solely responsible and liable for its content including but not limited to the views, representations, descriptions, statements, information, opinions and references ["Content"]. The Content of this book shall not constitute or be construed or deemed to reflect the opinion or expression of the Publisher or Editor. Neither the Publisher nor Editor endorse or approve the Content of this book or guarantee the reliability, accuracy or completeness of the Content published herein and do not make any representations or warranties of any kind, express or implied, including but not limited to the implied warranties of merchantability, fitness for a particular purpose. The Publisher and Editor shall not be liable whatsoever for any errors, omissions, whether such errors or omissions result from negligence, accident, or any other cause or claims for loss or damages of any kind, including without limitation, indirect or consequential loss or damage arising out of use, inability to use, or about the reliability, accuracy or sufficiency of the information contained in this book.

Made with ♥ on the Notion Press Platform
www.notionpress.com

I Dedicate this Book to my Parents and friends

Contents

1. Pdf To Excel Convertor   1

2. Excel To Pdf   3

3. Open Pdf   5

4. Editable Pdf   6

5. Pdf To Image   8

6. Pdf To Text   10

7. Pdf To Text   12

8. Split Pdf   13

9. Text Image TO Audio   15

10. Excel To CSV   17

11. Image To Pdf   19

12. Images To Video   21

13. Images To Powerpoint   23

14. Merge Videos   25

15. Pdf To Powerpoint   27

16. Video To Frames   30

## CHAPTER ONE

Pdf to Excel convertor

```python
import tkinter as tk
from tkinter import filedialog
import pdfplumber
import pytesseract
import pandas as pd
from PIL import Image
from PyPDF2 import PdfReader
import io
def pdf_to_excel():
root = tk.Tk()
root.withdraw()
# Select PDF file
file_path = filedialog.askopenfilename(title="Select a PDF File",
filetypes=[("PDF Files", "*.
if not file_path:
print("No file selected.")
return
extracted_data = []
# First try extracting tables from the PDF
with pdfplumber.open(file_path) as pdf:
for page in pdf.pages:
tables = page.extract_tables()
if tables:
for table in tables:
extracted_data.extend(table)
```

```python
# If no tables are found, extract text and apply OCR if needed
if not extracted_data:reader = PdfReader(file_path)
for page in reader.pages:
text = page.extract_text()
if text:
extracted_data.append([text]) # Store text in a list
# If no text is found, perform OCR
else:
for img in page.images:
img_data = img.data
img_obj = Image.open(io.BytesIO(img_data))
ocr_text = pytesseract.image_to_string(img_obj)
extracted_data.append([ocr_text]) # Store OCR result in a list
if not extracted_data:
print("No data extracted from the PDF.")
return
# Ask user for save location
output_excel_path                                                        =
filedialog.asksaveasfilename(defaultextension=".xlsx",
filetypes=[("Excel
if not output_excel_path:
print("Save location not selected.")
return
# Convert to DataFrame and save as Excel
df = pd.DataFrame(extracted_data)
df.to_excel(output_excel_path, index=False, header=False)
print(f"Excel file saved at: {output_excel_path}")
if __name__ == "__main__":
pdf_to_excel()
```

## CHAPTER TWO

Excel To Pdf

```python
import tkinter as tk
from tkinter import filedialog
import pandas as pd
from reportlab.lib.pagesizes import letter, landscape
from reportlab.pdfgen import canvas
def excel_to_pdf():
root = tk.Tk()
root.withdraw()
# Select an Excel file
file_path = filedialog.askopenfilename(title="Select an Excel File",
filetypes=[("Excel Files"
if not file_path:
print("No file selected.")
return# Read the Excel file
df = pd.read_excel(file_path)
# Ask user for save location
output_pdf_path                                                        =
filedialog.asksaveasfilename(defaultextension=".pdf",
filetypes=[("PDF Files
if not output_pdf_path:
print("Save location not selected.")
return
# Create a PDF
c = canvas.Canvas(output_pdf_path, pagesize=landscape(letter))
width, height = landscape(letter)
```

```python
# Set title
c.setFont("Helvetica-Bold", 14)
c.drawString(30, height - 30, "Excel to PDF Conversion")
# Write DataFrame content to PDF
c.setFont("Helvetica", 10)
x_offset = 30
y_offset = height - 60
# Column headers
for i, col_name in enumerate(df.columns):
c.drawString(x_offset + (i * 100), y_offset, str(col_name))
y_offset -= 20
# Row data (first 30 rows to avoid overflow)
for row in df.itertuples(index=False):
for i, value in enumerate(row):
c.drawString(x_offset + (i * 100), y_offset, str(value))
y_offset -= 15
if y_offset < 30:
c.showPage()
c.setFont("Helvetica", 10)
y_offset = height - 30
c.save()
print(f"PDF saved at: {output_pdf_path}")
if __name__ == "__main__":
excel_to_pdf()
```

## CHAPTER THREE

Open Pdf

```python
import fitz # PyMuPDF
from PIL import Image
import io
def extract_and_display_images(pdf_path):
doc = fitz.open(pdf_path) # Open the PDF file
for page_num, page in enumerate(doc, start=1):
images = page.get_images(full=True) # Extract images from the
page
if images:
for img_index, img in enumerate(images):
xref = img[0] # Image reference number
base_image = doc.extract_image(xref) # Extract image bytes
img_bytes = base_image["image"]
img_ext = base_image["ext"] # Image format (e.g., 'png', 'jpeg')
# Convert to PIL Image and display
image = Image.open(io.BytesIO(img_bytes))
image.show(title=f"Page {page_num} - Image {img_index+1}")
# Example Usage
extract_and_display_images("basics of electrical and electronic
enggineering.pdf")
```

## CHAPTER FOUR

Editable Pdf

```python
import tkinter as tk
from tkinter import filedialog
import pytesseract
from PIL import Image
from PyPDF2 import PdfReader, PdfWriter
from reportlab.pdfgen import canvas
import io
def convert_pdf_to_editable():
root = tk.Tk()
root.withdraw()
# Select a scanned PDF file
file_path = filedialog.askopenfilename(title="Select a PDF File",
filetypes=[("PDF Files", "*.
if not file_path:
print("No file selected.")
return
reader = PdfReader(file_path)
images = []
extracted_texts = []
# Extract images from the PDF
for page in reader.pages:for img in page.images:
img_data = img.data
img_obj = Image.open(io.BytesIO(img_data))
images.append(img_obj)
# Perform OCR on the image
```

```python
text = pytesseract.image_to_string(img_obj)
extracted_texts.append(text)
# Ask user for save location
output_pdf_path                                              =
filedialog.asksaveasfilename(defaultextension=".pdf",
filetypes=[("PDF Files
if not output_pdf_path:
print("Save location not selected.")
return
pdf_writer = PdfWriter()
# Create a text-based PDF with extracted text
text_pdf = output_pdf_path.replace(".pdf", "_text.pdf")
c = canvas.Canvas(text_pdf)
y_position = 800 # Initial Y position for text
for text in extracted_texts:
c.drawString(50, y_position, text[:100]) # Prevent text overflow
y_position -= 20
if y_position < 50: # Start new page if text exceeds limit
c.showPage()
y_position = 800
c.save()
# Merge original images with extracted text
for img in images:
img_path = "temp_img.pdf"
img.save(img_path, "PDF")
pdf_writer.append(img_path)
pdf_writer.append(text_pdf)
with open(output_pdf_path, "wb") as out_file:
pdf_writer.write(out_file)
print(f"Editable PDF saved at: {output_pdf_path}")
if __name__ == "__main__":
convert_pdf_to_editable()
```

## CHAPTER FIVE

Pdf To Image

```python
import os
import fitz # PyMuPDF
import tkinter as tk
from tkinter import filedialog
from PIL import Image
def select_pdf():
"""Open a file dialog to select a PDF file."""
root = tk.Tk()
root.withdraw() # Hide the root window
file_path    =    filedialog.askopenfilename(title="Select    a    PDF",
filetypes=[("PDF files", "*.pdf"))
return file_path
def select_output_folder():
"""Open a file dialog to select an output folder."""
root = tk.Tk()
root.withdraw()
folder_path = filedialog.askdirectory(title="Select Output Folder")
return folder_path
def convert_pdf_to_images():
"""Convert selected PDF to images and save in chosen folder."""
pdf_path = select_pdf()
if not pdf_path:print("No PDF selected!")
return
output_folder = select_output_folder()
if not output_folder:
```

```python
    print("No output folder selected!")
    return
try:
    # Open the PDF
    doc = fitz.open(pdf_path)
    # Convert each page to an image and save it
    for i, page in enumerate(doc):
        pix = page.get_pixmap(dpi=300) # Convert page to high-resolution image
        img = Image.frombytes("RGB", [pix.width, pix.height], pix.samples)
        img_path = os.path.join(output_folder, f"page_{i+1}.png")
        img.save(img_path, "PNG") # Save as PNG
        print(f"Saved: {img_path}")
    print("PDF successfully converted to images!")
except Exception as e:
    print(f"Error: {e}")
# Run the conversion
convert_pdf_to_images()
```

## CHAPTER SIX

Pdf To Text

```python
import tkinter as tk
from tkinter import filedialogimport pytesseract
from PIL import Image
from PyPDF2 import PdfReader, PdfWriter
from reportlab.pdfgen import canvas
import io
def convert_pdf_to_editable():
root = tk.Tk()
root.withdraw()
# Select a scanned PDF file
file_path = filedialog.askopenfilename(title="Select a PDF File",
filetypes=[("PDF Files", "*.
if not file_path:
print("No file selected.")
return
reader = PdfReader(file_path)
pdf_writer = PdfWriter()
extracted_texts = []
# Ask user for save location
output_pdf_path                                                        =
filedialog.asksaveasfilename(defaultextension=".pdf",
filetypes=[("PDF Files
if not output_pdf_path:
print("Save location not selected.")
return
```

```python
# Process each page
for i, page in enumerate(reader.pages):
# Extract text (for already searchable PDFs)
text = page.extract_text()
if not text:
# If no text is found, try OCR on images
for img in page.images:
img_data = img.data
img_obj = Image.open(io.BytesIO(img_data))
# Convert image to text using Tesseract OCR
ocr_text = pytesseract.image_to_string(img_obj)
extracted_texts.append(ocr_text)
extracted_texts.append(text if text else "")
# Keep original page in the new PDF
pdf_writer.add_page(page)
# Create a text-based PDF with extracted text
text_pdf   =   output_pdf_path.replace(".pdf",   "_text.pdf")c   =
canvas.Canvas(text_pdf)
y_position = 800 # Start position
for text in extracted_texts:
c.drawString(50, y_position, text[:100]) # Write only first 100
characters per line
y_position -= 20
if y_position < 50: # New page when needed
c.showPage()
y_position = 800
c.save()
# Merge extracted text PDF with the original PDF
pdf_writer.append(text_pdf)
with open(output_pdf_path, "wb") as out_file:
pdf_writer.write(out_file)
print(f"Editable PDF saved at: {output_pdf_path}")
if __name__ == "__main__":
convert_pdf_to_editable()
```

## CHAPTER SEVEN

Pdf To Text

```
import cv2
import os
from pdf2image import convert_from_path
def pdf_to_video(pdf_path, output_video, fps=1):
# Convert PDF pages to images
images = convert_from_path(pdf_path)
# Get image dimensions
width, height = images[0].size
# Define video codec and create VideoWriter
fourcc = cv2.VideoWriter_fourcc(*'mp4v') # or 'XVID'
video = cv2.VideoWriter(output_video, fourcc, fps, (width,
height))
for img in imagdef save_image(img, filename="temp.png"):
img.save(filename)
return filename
# Example usage
pdf_to_video("newpdffromtext.pdf", "output.mp4", fps=1)
```

## CHAPTER EIGHT

Split Pdf

```python
import os
from tkinter import Tk, filedialog
from PyPDF2 import PdfReader, PdfWriter
def split_pdf_into_parts(pdf_path, num_parts=10):
# Open the original PDF
reader = PdfReader(pdf_path)
total_pages = len(reader.pages)
# Calculate pages per part
pages_per_part = total_pages // num_parts
remainder = total_pages % num_parts
output_dir          =          os.path.join(os.path.dirname(pdf_path),
"Split_PDFs")
os.makedirs(output_dir, exist_ok=True)
start_page = 0
for i in range(num_parts):
writer = PdfWriter()
end_page = start_page + pages_per_part + (1 if i < remainder else
0)
for j in range(start_page, end_page):
writer.add_page(reader.pages[j])
output_file = os.path.join(output_dir, f"split_part_{i+1}.pdf")
with open(output_file, "wb") as out_pdf:
writer.write(out_pdf)
print(f"Saved: {output_file}")
start_page = end_page
```

```python
# Hide the Tkinter root window
Tk().withdraw()
# Open file dialog to select a PDF
pdf_path = filedialog.askopenfilename(title="Select a PDF File",
filetypes=[("PDF Files", "*.p
if pdf_path:
split_pdf_into_parts(pdf_path)print("PDF successfully split into
10 parts.")
else:
print("No file selected.")
```

## CHAPTER NINE

Text Image TO Audio

```python
import cv2
import pytesseract
import tkinter as tk
from tkinter import filedialog, messagebox
from PIL import Image
from gtts import gTTS
import os
import playsound
# Set Tesseract OCR path (Update path if needed)
pytesseract.pytesseract.tesseract_cmd = r"C:\Program Files\
Tesseract-OCR\tesseract.exe"
# Function to open file dialogdef select_file():
root = tk.Tk()
root.withdraw()
file_path = filedialog.askopenfilename(title="Select an Image File",
filetypes=[("Image Files", "*.png;*.jpg;*.jpeg;*.bmp")])
return file_path
# Function to extract text from image
def extract_text(image_path):
image = Image.open(image_path)
text = pytesseract.image_to_string(image)
return text.strip()
# Function to convert text to speech
def text_to_audio(text, audio_file="output.mp3"):
if not text:
```

```python
messagebox.showerror("Error", "No text found in image!")
return
tts = gTTS(text=text, lang="en")
tts.save(audio_file)
messagebox.showinfo("Success",    f"Audio    file    saved    as
{audio_file}")
# Play the audio file
playsound.playsound(audio_file)
# Main function
def main():
file_path = select_file()
if not file_path:
messagebox.showerror("Error", "No file selected!")
return
extracted_text = extract_text(file_path)
messagebox.showinfo("Extracted Text", extracted_text)
text_to_audio(extracted_text, "image_audio.mp3")
if __name__ == "__main__":
main()
```

## CHAPTER TEN

Excel To CSV

```python
import pandas as pd
import tkinter as tk
from tkinter import filedialog, messagebox
def convert_excel_to_csv():
"""Opens a file dialog to select an Excel file and converts it to
CSV."""
file_path = filedialog.askopenfilename(title="Select an Excel File",
filetypes=[("Excel Files"
if not file_path:
messagebox.showerror("Error", "No file selected!")
return
try:
df = pd.read_excel(file_path)
# Ask where to save the CSV file
save_path = filedialog.asksaveasfilename(defaultextension=".csv",
filetypes=[("CSV Files", "*.
if not save_path:
messagebox.showerror("Error", "No save location selected!")
return
df.to_csv(save_path, index=False)
messagebox.showinfo("Success", f"Excel file converted to CSV
successfully!\nSaved at: {save_pa
except Exception as e:
messagebox.showerror("Error", f"Failed to convert:\n{e}")
# Initialize GUI
```

```
root = tk.Tk()
root.withdraw() # Hide the main window
convert_excel_to_csv()
```

## CHAPTER ELEVEN

Image To Pdf

```
import cv2
import numpy as np
import pytesseract
import tkinter as tk
from tkinter import filedialog, messagebox
from PIL import Image
from reportlab.pdfgen import canvas
# Set up Tesseract OCR path (Change this if needed)
pytesseract.pytesseract.tesseract_cmd = r"C:\Program Files\
Tesseract-OCR\tesseract.exe"# Function to get file from dialog box
def select_file():
root = tk.Tk()
root.withdraw()
file_path = filedialog.askopenfilename(title="Select a Document
Image",
filetypes=[("Image Files", "*.png;*.jpg;*.jpeg;*.bmp")])
return file_path
# Function to process the image and extract text
def scan_document(image_path):
image = cv2.imread(image_path)
gray = cv2.cvtColor(image, cv2.COLOR_BGR2GRAY)
# Apply adaptive thresholding
processed = cv2.adaptiveThreshold(gray, 255,
cv2.ADAPTIVE_THRESH_GAUSSIAN_C,
```

```python
cv2.THRESH_BINARY, 11, 2)
return processed
# Function to extract text from image
def extract_text(image_path):
image = Image.open(image_path)
text = pytesseract.image_to_string(image)
return text.strip()
# Function to save the scanned document as PDF
def save_as_pdf(image, output_pdf):
h, w = image.shape
pdf = canvas.Canvas(output_pdf, pagesize=(w, h))
temp_image = "temp_scanned.jpg"
cv2.imwrite(temp_image, image)
pdf.drawImage(temp_image, 0, 0, width=w, height=h)
pdf.save()
messagebox.showinfo("Success", f"Scanned document saved as
{output_pdf}")
# Main function
def main():
file_path = select_file()
if not file_path:
messagebox.showerror("Error", "No file selected!")
return
scanned_image = scan_document(file_path)
# Show scanned document preview
cv2.imshow("Scanned Document", scanned_image)cv2.waitKey(0)
cv2.destroyAllWindows()
# Extract text
extracted_text = extract_text(file_path)
messagebox.showinfo("Extracted Text", extracted_text)
# Save as PDF
save_as_pdf(scanned_image, "scanned_document.pdf")
if __name__ == "__main__":
main
```

## CHAPTER TWELVE

Images To Video

```
import cv2
import os
import tkinter as tk
from tkinter import filedialog, messagebox
def create_video():
# Open file dialog to select multiple images
file_paths = filedialog.askopenfilenames(title="Select Images",
filetypes=[("Image Files", "*.
if not file_paths:
messagebox.showwarning("No Files Selected", "Please select at
least one image.")return
# Ask user where to save the video
output_path                                                       =
filedialog.asksaveasfilename(defaultextension=".mp4",
filetypes=[("MP4 Video", "
if not output_path:
return
try:
# Read the first image to get dimensions
first_image = cv2.imread(file_paths[0])
height, width, layers = first_image.shape
# Create VideoWriter object
fourcc = cv2.VideoWriter_fourcc(*'mp4v') # Codec for MP4
video = cv2.VideoWriter(output_path, fourcc, 1, (width, height)) #
1 FPS video
```

```python
# Add images to video
for image_path in file_paths:
img = cv2.imread(image_path)
img_resized = cv2.resize(img, (width, height)) # Ensure all images
have the same size
video.write(img_resized)
# Release the video
video.release()
messagebox.showinfo("Success",          f"Video          saved
at:\n{output_path}")
except Exception as e:
messagebox.showerror("Error", f"Failed to create video:\n{e}")
# Create GUI
root = tk.Tk()
root.withdraw() # Hide the main window
create_video()
```

## CHAPTER THIRTEEN

Images To Powerpoint

```python
import tkinter as tk
from tkinter import filedialog
from pptx import Presentation
from pptx.util import Inches
import os
def open_image_dialog():
try:
# Open a file dialog to select multiple images
file_paths = filedialog.askopenfilenames(title="Select Images",
filetypes=[("Image files", "*.
if file_paths:
create_ppt(file_paths)
except Exception as e:
print(f"Error in open_image_dialog: {e}")
def create_ppt(image_paths):
try:
# Create a PowerPoint presentation
prs = Presentation()
# Loop through each image and add it as a slide in the PowerPoint
presentation
for image_path in image_paths:
slide = prs.slides.add_slide(prs.slide_layouts[5]) # Blank slide
layout
slide.shapes.add_picture(image_path, Inches(0), Inches(0),
width=Inches(10), height=Inches(7.5
```

```python
print(f"Added {image_path} to slide")
# Save the presentation
pptx_path = "output_presentation.pptx"
prs.save(pptx_path)
print(f"PowerPoint presentation saved as {pptx_path}")except
Exception as e:
print(f"Error in create_ppt: {e}")
def main():
try:
# Create a basic Tkinter window
root = tk.Tk()
root.title("Image to PowerPoint Converter")
# Hide the main window
root.withdraw()
# Open the file dialog to select images
open_image_dialog()
# Keep the window open until the dialog is closed
root.mainloop()
except Exception as e:
print(f"Error in main: {e}")
if __name__ == "__main__":
main()
```

## CHAPTER FOURTEEN

Merge Videos

```
import os
import subprocess
import tkinter as tk
from tkinter import filedialog, messageboxdef merge_videos():
root = tk.Tk()
root.withdraw() # Hide main window
file_paths = filedialog.askopenfilenames(title="Select Videos to
Merge", filetypes=[("Video Fi
if not file_paths:
messagebox.showerror("Error", "No videos selected!")
return
# Ask for output file
output_file = filedialog.asksaveasfilename(title="Save Merged
Video As", defaultextension=".mp
filetypes=[("MP4 File", "*.mp4")])
if not output_file:
messagebox.showerror("Error", "No output file specified!")
return
# Convert all videos to a common format to ensure smooth merging
converted_videos = []
for i, file in enumerate(file_paths):
temp_output = f"temp_video_{i}.mp4"
command = [
"ffmpeg", "-i", file, "-c:v", "libx264", "-c:a", "aac", "-strict",
"experimental",
```

```python
        "-preset", "fast", "-y", temp_output
    ]
    subprocess.run(command, stdout=subprocess.DEVNULL, stderr=subprocess.DEVNULL)
    converted_videos.append(temp_output)
# Create a temporary text file listing all input videos
temp_list_file = "video_list.txt"
with open(temp_list_file, "w", encoding="utf-8") as f:
    for file in converted_videos:
        f.write(f"file '{file}'\n")
# Merge videos using FFmpeg
command = ["ffmpeg", "-f", "concat", "-safe", "0", "-i", temp_list_file, "-c", "copy", output_
try:
    subprocess.run(command, check=True)
    messagebox.showinfo("Success", f"Videos merged successfully!\nSaved as: {output_file}")
except subprocess.CalledProcessError:
    messagebox.showerror("Error", "Failed to merge videos. Please check FFmpeg installation.")
# Clean up temporary files
os.remove(temp_list_file)
for temp_file in converted_videos:
    os.remove(temp_file)# Run the function
merge_videos()
```

## CHAPTER FIFTEEN

Pdf To Powerpoint

```
import tkinter as tk
from tkinter import filedialog
from pdf2image import convert_from_path
from pptx import Presentation
from pptx.util import Inches
import timedef open_pdf_dialog():
try:
# Open a file dialog to select a PDF file
file_path = filedialog.askopenfilename(title="Select Scanned PDF",
filetypes=[("PDF files", "*
if file_path:
images = convert_pdf_to_images(file_path)
create_ppt(images)
except Exception as e:
print(f"Error in open_pdf_dialog: {e}")
def convert_pdf_to_images(pdf_path):
try:
# Convert the selected PDF to images
print(f"Converting {pdf_path} to images...")
# Convert the entire PDF to images, but process each page one-by-
one with a delay
pages = convert_from_path(pdf_path, 150) # DPI set to 150 (You
can adjust this for quality/pe
total_pages = len(pages)
print(f"Total pages to convert: {total_pages}")
```

```python
# Save each page as an image
image_paths = []
for i, page in enumerate(pages, start=1):
image_path = f"page_{i}.png"
page.save(image_path, 'PNG')
image_paths.append(image_path)
print(f"Saved {image_path}")
# Optional: Add a delay if necessary
time.sleep(1) # Adjust this time to make it slower or faster
return image_paths
except Exception as e:
print(f"Error in convert_pdf_to_images: {e}")
return []
def create_ppt(image_paths):
try:
# Create a PowerPoint presentation
prs = Presentation()
# Loop through each image and add it as a slide in the PowerPoint
presentation
for image_path in image_paths:
slide = prs.slides.add_slide(prs.slide_layouts[5]) # Blank slide
layout
slide.shapes.add_picture(image_path,    Inches(0),    Inches(0),
width=Inches(10), height=Inches(7.5
print(f"Added {image_path} to slide")# Save the presentation
pptx_path = "output_presentation.pptx"
prs.save(pptx_path)
print(f"PowerPoint presentation saved as {pptx_path}")
except Exception as e:
print(f"Error in create_ppt: {e}")
def main():
try:
# Create a basic Tkinter window
root = tk.Tk()
root.title("Scanned PDF to PowerPoint Converter")
```

```python
    # Hide the main window
    root.withdraw()
    # Open the file dialog to select the scanned PDF
    open_pdf_dialog()
    # Keep the window open until the dialog is closed
    root.mainloop()
except Exception as e:
    print(f"Error in main: {e}")
if __name__ == "__main__":
    main()
```

## CHAPTER SIXTEEN

Video To Frames

```
import cv2
import os
import tkinter as tk
from tkinter import filedialog, simpledialog, messagebox
def extract_frames():
root = tk.Tk()
root.withdraw() # Hide the root window
# Select video file
video_path = filedialog.askopenfilename(title="Select Video File",
filetypes=[("Video Files",
if not video_path:
messagebox.showerror("Error", "No video selected!")
return
# Ask where to save frames
save_folder = filedialog.askdirectory(title="Select Folder to Save
Frames")
if not save_folder:
messagebox.showerror("Error", "No save folder selected!")
return
# Ask for frame extraction interval
interval = simpledialog.askinteger("Frame Interval", "Extract every
Nth frame (e.g., 10 for ev
if not interval:
messagebox.showerror("Error", "Invalid interval!")
return
```

```python
# Open video and extract frames
cap = cv2.VideoCapture(video_path)
frame_count = 0
saved_count = 0
while cap.isOpened():
ret, frame = cap.read()
if not ret:
break # Stop if the video ends
if frame_count % interval == 0: # Save every Nth frame
frame_filename                =                os.path.join(save_folder,
f"frame_{saved_count:04d}.jpg")
cv2.imwrite(frame_filename, frame)
saved_count += 1
frame_count += 1
cap.release()
messagebox.showinfo("Success",          f"Frames          extracted
successfully!\nSaved  {saved_count}  frames  toif  __name__  ==
"__main__":
extract_frames()
```

www.ingramcontent.com/pod-product-compliance
Lightning Source LLC
Chambersburg PA
CBHW020347180726
47991CB00021B/3039